C-Suite Mentor Diaries
Collection of Articles
by Dhananjaya Parkhe on Linkedin Pulse

Dhananjay Parkhe

1st Edition
Getting Started
Dhananjaya Parkhe published his articles on LInkedin Pulse for nearly a year. The Collection of these articles are divided into different subjects in eBooks for Kindle and Paperbacks like this one is collection of articles on C-Suite. I am sure the aspiring C-LEVEL executives and those already in the C-Suite as Executives and those aspiring for Supervisory Board level positions will find the advice and learnings from my experience useful.

My writing style has Humor as base and borders on Satirical yet, I hope you would enjoy reading. My mentees tell me that they like it. In my early School/ College days and for few years of working life I did Poetry and was nicknamed as "Corporate Bard". In literary studies and rhetoric, the style of writing I used then was extravagant, heavily ornamented, and/or bizarre. The term more commonly used to characterize in the visual arts and music, baroque (sometimes capitalized- BAROQUE) can also refer to a highly ornate style of prose or poetry. That was Me! Enjoy!

CEO's Diet Diary 1
Diet, Gurus, Best sellers and Me...
Humor in C Suite

I remember a session with a renowned Coaching Guru who once said, that the sure Best Seller he'd write next will have 'Diet' as its catchy Headline☺

I have in the past 10 years had several encounters (?) with Diabetes Educators, Diet Management Teachers, Dietitians and several others who work with my Diabetes Doctors or Endocrinologists and who take over the task of explaining the task of HOW to manage my weight after the Doctor has prescribed Medicines and / or Insulin dose.

Now the fact is I was always a Heavy child and also a heavier side young man and as my travel days on Motor bike started getting replaced with Travel by Air (since 1991) I began to put on even more weight. Not just the weight of my position, responsibility but physical too☺

As I Crossed 60th Year last year and came in the Senior Citizen category automatically (for Income Tax purpose ☺) a friend sent me a Link to a web page with several One-Liners on my Physical and Mental state☺ . I especially liked the ones below:

1. You can eat dinner at 4 P.M.

2. You enjoy hearing about other people's operations.

3. People call at 9 PM and ask, 'Did I wake you?'

4. Your investment in health insurance is finally beginning to pay off. 5. I joined a health club last year, spent about 4000 bucks.

Haven't lost a Kilo. Apparently, you should go there!

And few on my New-found habit of Walking which I took up post retirement two years ago - what with a Nike Apps to Match which sends a Tweet, FB message and updates Instagram with my 'Running (?)" Diagram every day.

A. I should exercise early in the morning before my brain figures out what I'm doing.

B. I like long walks, especially when they are taken by people who annoy me.

C. I have flabby thighs, but fortunately my stomach covers them.

D. The advantage of exercising every day is that you die healthier.

E. If you are going to try cross-country skiing, start with a small country.

So, what I do is to check my Weight on a Digital scale daily. Check my BP and record in a Note book. Check my Sugars Empty on Stomach and 2 hours after the Breakfast. Record my Temperature and Pulse rate. That makes my wife and the Doctors happy. It also saves me a Daily Fee of Rs. 800 for the Nurse - as I use self-help ☺. Doctor gives it a Monthly cursory glance and asks me (as a retired Corporate professional) with raised eyebrows - "Any aberrations from Normal?" WOW! I feel like charging him my Hourly Fee for the waiting Room waiting time as well. (Doctors are never prompt in calling you at the appointment time - I have realized now).

But I have digressed a little (or perhaps too much) - don't mind some of these 'Senior Moments' the Baby boomers and those around them should go thru ☺.

So I was talking about the Diet Gurus and the young ladies/assistants who help the Doctors with the unpleasant task of making me follow a Diet Regime. The Doctors are great when it comes to delegating the troublesome part. The good thing with them is they must simply see reports - they are not even required to touch the patients. Get this report, get that report and see me in a week. Add half a tablet or reduce one or add 4 units of insulin or reduce some is what they indulge into. And the poor Dietitians have to face logical questions (remember - there never are stupid questions !! only stupid answers. he he he ☺.

Most of the doctors have some posters about the Good food, balanced food, attributes of food, vegetables and fruits made by school children and rank bad artists around their room. The Dietitians usually are armed with " Your Diet Plan for the Day" sheet even if they are going to prescribe it for 6-8 weeks for you! They also come armed with poorly written foods you cannot eat and foods you can eat. Even the eat part contains many tips what you cannot eat.

They are taught to ask you what you like to eat and say - Stop eating that! What do you start your day with - STOP That!! What do you eat for Breakfast - STOP That! And if you have done the mistake of taking your wife along - be sure, that she will follow the advice in LETTER and SPIRIT making you think - "Do I really exist to EAT or EAT to Exist?" And THEN I had my second cardiac stroke (THIS wasn't Silent like the previous one) - " was it better to come out of unconsciousness? to what gain? To Not Eat?"

I find it amusing that these young Dietitians surviving on Half a Liter of Water and wanting me to do so too. Second time you meet a new one - she tells you to drink 6-10 liters as the prior one gave you a wrong suggestion and it gave you Constipation! And she is armed with a leaflet to boot which describes this diet Plan???

My last encounters were interesting and gave me some great business ideas as well. I said to the Doc who happened to be with the Dietitian for some reason and she said "1 Chapatti for Lunch/ Dinner - you must be starving and bored! " At last, I found empathy and understanding. I just wished that many more Docs like her take such interest in patients. I remember as Agra/ Vet medicine student, we were often taken to the Stables in the College and we'd be required to examine the Patients (Animals). Unfortunately, our patients could not talk. Here the Humans as patients can talk but aren't allowed to find voice under the pressure of your Diseases, the aura around the doctors, the Reports as Factual evidences etc. but to make you go quiet and obedient, disciplined in front of rank junior / Learner Dietitians - I found the idea remotely laughable.

So, I found a new thought, a business idea! I am an obedient patient and I do exactly as my doctors and their juniors prescribe me including my wife and her influencers' who advise her regularly with supplements (for e.g. bitter gourd juice - just to name a few) and I respond well to treatment. And, I don't mean 'TREATMENT' as a Human Patient - don't mistake me please.

I remember an HR friend who was also an NLP expert (Neuro Linguistic Programming expert). He once said to me - ' You, Jay! You Don't HAVE to eat so much!" It was a very powerful message indeed. 10 Years ago, I used it to stop Drinking Alcohol. Also, stopped all form of Non-Vegetarian Food. Managed over the years my weight from 125 Kilos to 92.5 currently and am willing to drop more! I used the same Prompt to stop Smoking habit of 48 years in Feb 2014. And there lies the idea!

How about training the Dietitians in the following ways?

A. Teaching them to ask the Right Questions.

B. Making them more sensitive to the patients and their past efforts at Dieting.

C Learning to Compliment for good efforts.

D. Stopping to throw up ready-made literatures at one a sundry without any regard to specific conditions of the patient AND

E. Finally, teaching some NLP techniques and powerful words like the one I quoted above from my HR friend whose words remind me of TREATMENT and Second and most important a Very Powerful message delivery right into my Brain where there is ready acceptance to change a Habit at once!

The Baby Boomers are a Retiring lot but I am sure, someone reading this article may see this as a Start Up training opportunity of Teaching NLP and Empathy to the Future Generation of the Diet Gurus and I hope their generation flourishes and is very successful.

C-CSO Diaries 2

Loyalty to Marketer or the King (customer)?

C Suite Mentoring

Whenever someone says 'Loyalty' it reminds me of the time I was on CLM project. My Question always was - If the Customer is the (proverbial) King - should he be Loyal or the people serving him should be Loyal to him.

I came across a good Picture Quote by the Former President of India which read "Love Your Job, You don't have to Love your company! For you may not know when your company may stop Loving you!" So, True, these words in these times of rampant Re-orgy (Sorry, Re-organization), Re-Strum (Re-structuring), Dowsed (Down Sizing), Rigs (Right Sizing) which HR function is constantly required to do while bulk recruiting!

I also saw this Picture Quote which said " Respect is Earned, Honesty is Appreciated, Trust is Gained and Loyalty is Returned!" I was shocked - Loyalty seems to be a 'thing' which you receive and return? Then I remembered, the CLM questions we framed for the project:

1. Would you use our service again? was the Loyalty Question.

2. Would you recommend our service to someone known? was the Customer Satisfaction question in the list of nearly 40 questions

I hope, you're getting the drift! So, whether we do an Employee Satisfaction Survey or a Customer Satisfaction (Loyalty) survey the idea is to get 'something' in return from the customer (of course, other than the money for the services rendered) that is Customer's Loyalty.

From the Employees, the questions are differently phrased though. They are not asked whether they'd like to come back and work for the company again? Although, if you are the employee Referee you are asked this time and again by recruiters - whether you'd like to have this employee back? I wonder why?

And to end, this short discourse about Loyalty - Companies these days offer to existing employees - Get a Buddy Incentive thereby saving some recruitment costs - Isn't that Employer's (The King's) Loyalty? A way of returning Loyalty. Do feel free to give me a word of your worthy advice and a Feedforward, I'd very much appreciate it. Rather than these Marketer created Ladders to climb I would rather say - King is Dead - Long Live the King.

Post Retirement C-Suite Diaries 3
61 Today and a few more to Go...
Humor in C Suite

Years ago, Palmistry, Astrology, Horoscopes, Face Reading, Thumb Reading was a passion for me as School/ College Student. At my first jobs in sales they became ' ice-breakers'! More later, as I began recruiting - it helped me to learn Human beings and their profiles more intimately. Many HR models and predictive models like - MBTI, Thomas Profiling, Strengths finder etc. became my favorites. I realized that apart from my own future, I was also very keen to gain insights into my customers, my co-workers, my juniors and seniors!

The passion continues and I have given in to Technology now. I still love Biorhythm and have the Apps installed on my Mac and my iPhone ever since I found them. I read a book about them years ago and became a fan.

"Dear Jay, this is your Biorhythm for Sunday, April 6th:"

Yes. It's a great day, I turn 61 today.

"Today your intellectual level is 90%: you will be a leader in the workplace."

In India, you become a Senior Citizen at 60, just by living that many years! :D. And No, I am no more a workplace leader in any MNC - I am still a workplace leader at my small work-desk-station!

"Your physical level is 2%: it is advisable to avoid muscular effort. This may be true, what with the Two strokes in past 4 months and still on Medication, Meditation and Yoga exercises."

"Your emotional level is 0%: it is worth putting off delicate matters!"

I suppose, I should take this seriously and write something with a bit of humor, isn't it?

Today's Biorhythm Chart looks like this. Click.

My Tarot reading says:

"Everything seems to be happening so fast now that you don't even have time to think about what you're going to do; you simply do it. "

Yes. I liked this. That's what I'm doing.

"You barely complete a conversation or finish a project before something new comes at you from another direction. "

Yes. True. Many friends sending Greetings on every possible Social Media Network and emails, iPhone, Landline etc. etc. I am happy and grateful to acknowledge all Greetings. This is my Day and my Friends - You Made It My Day!

"Fortunately, you are a master at thinking on your feet and reacting quickly. No planning is necessary today; you can always adjust later. Give yourself permission to embrace the spontaneity of the moment. "

That was easier said than done Dear Tarot interpreter! :D

I also Read inching of the Day:

Tung Jen: Fellowship,

"To achieve your aims, you must unite with virtuous people. Indeed, it will be easier to reach every objective if a group of individuals (albeit of different characters), had the same common goal. However always keep your own personality and act so that you enrichen one another."

What I wish to do in the 62nd Year are:

1. Revive my old hobby of Freehand Drawing like the one on

left. I hope my Mentors would bless me.

2. Write some good, some humorous articles here to make your day enjoyable, my readers! Publish an ebook or two, make a video/podcast and share it on a MOOC learning website for Free !

CMO Diaries 4

Most Powerful Skill is Networking?
C Suite Mentoring

"Your ability to connect is going to be the most powerful skill in the world" - Larry Benet

You've Made It. You are in the C Suite. Your Image consultant, your advertising consultant are saying 'It is cliché', it is the 'IN THING' to be on a Social Media Network or on a Professional Network. You need to be visible to the Public, Customers, Stake holders and perhaps to the headhunters too - (you may hire ghost writers if the in-feed in your Inbox is too high). You are flooded with advice. So, you join Twitter. (I just read 44% of the Twitterati have not Tweeted Even Once - Wow! Isn't it).

Some of you may make a profile on LinkedIn. Very few of you join Facebook. Tech Savvy among you who have some passions for subjects like photography may also use a nom de plume and post photos to Flickr or Picasa. Only the serious photographers may post to National Geographic. I have met few serious CEO photography enthusiasts who could make it their second profession. Or on a sabbatical leave, they would be happy shooting! Pictures and Movies, I mean it.

"To achieve great things, two things are needed; a plan, and not quite enough time" - said Leonard Bernstein.

As a C Suite Member you may need some support with the first i.e. Plan - the Second - you have it in very acute supply. You may read a good article here.

Here is what I do after years of Networking experience of Trials and Errors and getting mentor support when I was a Newbie Networkers.

1. I began learning to network spending between 6-12 hours on slow speed modems and very slow Internet. I wanted to connect with people in different countries. I learnt I had to be around to have a live chat, dialogue in their Time Zone. Not simple, I know. It was my first phase of learning to Network.

2. Joining Groups/ Creating Groups in areas where either we are Specialists or Experts or we have a wish to be one or we would like to read interactive communications between experts on matters of some interest to us. LinkedIn initially, did not have a limit - today there is a limit of 50 group you can create or join. These provided me an opportunity to learn and share. I chose CSR, Ethics, Public Policy, Public Affairs, Recruiting, Leadership, Anti-Corruption, Integrity groups to name a few.

3. Appreciate, Applaud - Whether we like it or Not, all of us have an 'Applause factor' - the 'Receiving Pat on our backs factor'. We like to have 'Feedback' and as Dr. Marshall Goldsmith teaches - 'Feedforward factor' which are so critical in our life. I spend about 15 minutes every morning sending Birthday greetings, Work Anniversary greetings, Profile changes (usually

a new gig, a promotion, a move to a new place) to people in my network. Sometimes you get a response, some don't bother to even say 'Thank you' - they are my 'Time Savers' - they go out of my network in a process I call as 'Empty the Cup - to have a Refill' or in more agonistic language - " It is my Shrink to Grow Network Strategy". Try it. It brings people closer and creates an opportunity to filter your network of unnecessary trash you acquire by accepting every invitation to connect.

4. I like Linkedin Pulse and the Influencer articles. I may not get a chance to connect with the writers, yet I try to follow them and read a series of their articles to understand where are they coming from, consistency of their thoughts and my own alignment - likes, dislikes, learnings. Sometimes, I comment - generally to appreciate or to seek a clarification. These are great online learning tools connecting me with greatly experienced people with a great deal of knowledge acquired with wealth of experience. This is my Treasure.

5. "The tragedy of life is not death, but what we let die inside of us while we live." - Norman Cousins said.

I feel, utilizing our time in C Suite and later to SHARE our knowledge and experience, networking, mentoring, writing articles, essays, answering questions is a great way to live - before we die. As I said earlier, we need a plan and we are very short of time.

"The most powerful drive in the ascent of a man is his pleasure in his own skill. He loves to do what he does well and, having done it well, he loves to do it better "Jacob Grotowski

C-Suite CHRO/CPO Diaries 5
Are HR Interventions Meddling?
C-Suite Mentoring

I joined NHRDN in 1993 to learn HR. What motivated me was a lecture I attended there on a friend's invitation about " Predictive Techniques in HR" and that thrilled me. As a Headhunter, Retained Search Consultant then, I felt, I could recruit Performing/ Predictable Stars and have a great run with my Top Line and manage the bottom Lines in P&L well.

Over the years, I came to hate a word most HR literate people used which I found agonistic enough to generate hatred in me: Remember, my newfound love for HR was due also to the First question " Why people behave the way they do" (which is still unanswered BTW) apart from the Performance Predictability

The Definition of the Word **"Intervention"** found on the web says : "An intervention is an orchestrated attempt by one or many people – usually family and friends – to get someone to seek professional help with an addiction or some kind of traumatic event or crisis, or other serious problem. The term intervention is most often used when the traumatic event involves addiction to drugs or other items. Intervention can also refer to the act of using a similar technique within a therapy session. Interventions have been used to address serious personal problems, including, but not limited to, alcoholism, compulsive gambling, drug abuse, compulsive eating and other eating disorders, self-harm and being the victim of abuse."

For some reason, I found Success, Top Performance and Winning as Events, Addictive but never meeting the criterion for being used at the workplace by Learned HR people and their favorite consultants to come and take people thru the 'Performance Management Intervention (sorry they used the term ' Initiative' PMI) to do what they felt Right i.e. HR Interventions.

I also came across another word - **Meddlesome! Meddlesome?** Where else? In the Dictionary! Meddlesome adjective \'me-dell-sum\: interfering with the activities and concerns of other people in an unwanted or unwelcome way: inclined to meddle Full Definition of MEDDLESOME   given to meddling — meddlesomeness noun

See meddlesome defined for English-language learners » See meddlesome defined for kids » Examples of MEDDLESOME

1. Her neighbors saw her as a meddlesome nuisance. Me as General Manager, Profit Centre Head I found HR neighbors similarly.

2. <meddlesome neighbors kept asking the couple when they were going to have children>. The Team members especially in Indoor and outdoor Sales teams thought similarly.

You can study Synonyms busy, interfering, intruding, intrusive, meddling, nosy (or nosey), obtrusive, officious, presuming, presumptuous, protrusive, prying, pushing, pushy, snoopy if you like ☺

They were different adjectives most of my direct reports and juniors would use in One-on-One meetings or in parties we organized for the staff.:

(Antonyms for Meddlesome is unobtrusive and HR secretly having that ambition that they'd be some day 'Equal Business Partners' of the CEO thought - this is their Birthright!

You can read about Related words bold, brazen, bumptious, impertinent, impudent, insolent, rude; invading, trespassing; curious, inquisitive; annoying, harassing, pestiferous; overbearing, super serviceable, choice is yours ☺

One of the favorite words for HR was **'Feedback'** which crept into organizations when some HR guys came back from a 10 days International training seminar.

The Related words were indeed expected to be given as ' FEEDFORWARD' by their team=mates which they politely refrained.: P And there were some Near Antonyms which possibly described the HR functions and consultants engaged by them for PERFORMANCE MANAGEMENT and impotent INTERVENTIONS Thank you for being patient and reading.

If you read more about words like hands-off; uninvolved; quiet, reclusive, reserved, reticent, retiring, silent, taciturn, withdrawn; inhibited, restrained, subdued; you will probably empathise with me ☺ !

CLM is something Else- Diaries 6
C L M Alienation/ Alignment.
C Suite Mentoring

CLM - Customer Loyalty Measurement - the conventional abbreviation.

CLM- Career Limiting Move/s another abbreviation, I learnt the hard way ☺

We discuss today:

CLM with this new meaning which needs our deep understanding in C-LEVEL with terms like - Alignment and Alienation.

We all know, a corporate board has three Key responsibilities:

1. They set overall strategy,

2. They hire the right CEO, and

3. They put in place compensation systems that create alignment in the agency relationship with owners.

Achieving alignment means:

1. Ensure that your goals,

2. your team's goals, and the

3. organization's goals are all in alignment.

In my experience, Creation of Alignment by the C Suite Member/ CEO goes beyond just putting in place a compensation system. I have seen in transitory phases when new CEOs take command, many CEOs are focused towards creating alignment in the organization and fail by ending up creating Alienation within the organization. Some of them are obsessed with Words like FOCUS, ALIGNMENT and fail to understand the Human Dynamics and People element. (In my experience, I found much later – these politician CEOs actually were looking for loyal juniors – YES MEN in short – nothing else ☺).

While CEOs in C-Suite tries to improve Business Alignment and People Performance to drive breakthrough results for companies of all sizes; Alienation can be a **Critical Limiting facto**r to Success and Achievement of Goals.

So, what is Alienation? I read somewhere " I don't want to express alienation. It isn't what I feel. I'm interested in various kinds of passionate engagement. All my work says be serious, be passionate, wake up."

An example of usage in Corporate world (of the word Alienation is given as) "After the employee was not chosen for a recent promotion at his company, he felt a sense of alienation from his management."

The Term Alienation thus Means : (From Human resource management perspective) : A Sense of estrangement felt by employees, reflected in their lack of warmth towards the organization and

1. basic <u>decision making</u>,

2. lack of human contact,

3. little hope for betterment, and a feeling of powerlessness.

These can become severely limiting factors in the path of Achievement of the Goals.

Alienation can, thus, derail the CEO from his goal. The Term Alienation Means: (From Human resource management perspective):

- A Sense of estrangement felt by employees,

- reflected in their lack of warmth towards the organization and

- in believing that their job/work is not meaningful

- to other aspects of their lives

Thus, when Alienation begins to happen - not just the Alignment - the Goals themselves are under Risk. A Prudent CEO/ C Suite member would not just understand the Critical Success Factors; they would also do well to understand the Critical Limiting Factors such as Alienation lest they prove to be their Career Limiting Factors.

CMD/ Chairman Diaries 7
Does Elastic Leadership mean Rubber Spine?
C Suite Mentoring

Defining Elasticity: A measure of a variable's sensitivity to a change in another variable. In economics, elasticity refers the degree to which individuals (consumers/producers) change their demand/amount supplied in response to price or income changes. Calculated as:

Investopedia explains Elasticity:

Elasticity is used to assess the change in consumer demand because of a change in the good's price. When the value is greater than 1, this suggests that the demand for the good/service is affected by the price, whereas a value that is less than 1 suggest that the demand is insensitive to price.

Businesses often strive to sell/market products or services that are or seem inelastic in demand because doing so can mean that few customers will be lost because of price increases.

The C-Suite Players on one had must understand the Price, Demand and Elasticity as a part of their Commercial Acumen what I wish to discuss today is about a Behavior Elasticity. I like watching TV serials like " The Practice" and "Boston Legal". I come across many legal cases where in cases of homicide the Lawyers take a position describing the act as 'Temporary insanity' when the Accused "Snapped". I refer to this state as Mental or behavioral Elasticity.

This occurs to Executives at many points. Take the Annual Appraisal phase for one. One of my Mentees who was to go thru the Annual Appraisal process said to me that he'd like to discuss his future options very soon. He is a Top performer, quite a consistent one at that. My only suggestion was that ' Your Elastic is Stretched, Performance Stretch Bonus has stretched it further, don't let it snap. You've come to me - I know the 'Break Point' - Let me provide "Two Palm support" at this break point and stop it from snapping with emotional support. Speak to me in a week's time - if you still require a Decision-making support and either you've let the Elastic rubber band of your behavior snap or break or you still feel under tremendous pressure. In 99% of such cases, I know my mentees do not look for any Decision support from me. They do appreciate the emotional support - "the Two Palm support system" I tend to provide as mentor which is to help them counter their Temporary insanity moments being avoided in the short term.

Which brings me to another point. ' Does Performance has a Lifecycle like a Product's Life Cycle?' While all organizations want only 'Stars' and consistent performers - I have sometimes felt in my working life that we fail to notice the ' Decline phase of the Performance Life Cycle phase soon enough' and neither provide mentor support not provide the ' Two Palm support' of a Mentor.

Thus, most Key Performance Indicators are likely to become 'Key Perishable Indicators' for many executives including those in the C Suite :). Well! That's my theory and I am conscious that a 'Theory is nothing but One Man's Opinion' :),

"A faerie heart is different from a human heart. Human hearts are elastic. They have room for all sorts of passions, and they can break and heal and love again and again. Faerie hearts are evolutionarily less sophisticated. They are small and hard, like tiny grains of sand. Our hearts are too small to love more than one person in a lifetime." — Jodi Lynn Anderson (Tiger Lily)

To Achieve 'Sustainable' Performance i.e. consistent High level of Performance and recognize the 'Performance Life Cycle' of ourselves or our juniors what should Elastic Leadership do?

- Elastic leadership is a word used by me here in team context. It's about leading a team differently, based on your discovery of the Team's Performance Life Cycle Stage. These phases can change from day to day or week to week. Establishing right measures can help us keep adapting to the new phase, or we will keep them at 'Breakpoint' constantly.

- Elastic Leadership is about transforming the Team. From chaotic results to learning and moving from learning to self-leading phases quickly.

"When a great truth once gets abroad in the world, no power on earth can imprison it, or prescribe its limits, or suppress it. It is bound to go on till it becomes the thought of the world." Unknown author

No, I don't Mean the Elastic Leadership to be one which is like Rubber Spine or one which comes to break point all the time. I do mean, Flexibility and Resilience and I do mean Consistency and Persistent type.

CHRO/CPO Diary Again 8

Employee Loyalty - My Foot!
REALLY My Foot! ☺

I followed a convention, a family convention - I joined a Bank at 21. Slight departure from what my parents did - worked for the Government for life. So, when I changed to a Sales role in a Public-Sector company - I was a 'Different guy' in the family. So much so, when I went to see a would be bride for myself the would-be father in law commented - ' You do a thankless, unstable job' and refused to marry his daughter with me ☺. Thank God he blessed me (I am now happily married with my wife and my late Father in law a banker was a true friend, philosopher an guide to me). So, when I moved to a managerial career or when I decided to be an entrepreneur and failed at this and rejoined an MNC - it was Rebel behavior because my family consisted of Loyal Servants to the Government and many indeed served in Bureaucrats / Armed Forces / Educators!

I remember going to my B School for recruitment and asked the Respected Director who was my mentor that I'd like to recruit from a Part Time Management Course batch, someone with experience - someone very much like me - he flat refused and said - 'We don't produce any more Parkhe's here!" I took that as compliment. Year was mid 90's and the students were taught –

" First year will go in learning and Mastering the Trade and moving up. Second Year (if you are still in the company) would be when you're at peak of your performance and growing - may be bypassing and climbing 2-3 ladders at the same time. Third year (And, if you are with the same company) it is because at 30-34 you are on the 'Fast Track' and 'On List' to be the MD/CEO and sure enough, you are not bored - otherwise it is time to quit. Forget Loyalty of the MBAs.

The scenario changed to ever better (or worse!) in the early 21st Century when being in the company for 12-18 months was looked down by your Peer Group :). Do you remember?

Changing Horizon of HR is quite interesting and intriguing. I was reading few HR profiles recently which described themselves as: "Talent Sustainability; Onboarding, Engagement, Bench Strength, and Learning Systems". Quite a transformation, I must say from HR of 20 years ago!

With this for Fresh MBAs and their learning from B Schools How important, then is Employee Loyalty in current times?

I remember a friend of my uncle who was once a Finance Minister of Gujrat said to me in 1979 said to me that he left the Grand Old Party because the Leader demanded Personal Loyalty from him which he refused. Joined hands with Rebels and formed the First Non-Congress Government in the State of Gujrat.

Here is what he said

"In my scheme of Politics of today: Loyalty to Ideals comes First, Loyalty to Institution comes Next and Loyalty to Individuals comes Last".

Alas! Politics of today has reversed the order of Priorities today. The Contemporary political parties believe in Loyalty to Individuals and Dynasties First and have no place for the Ideals. But that apart.

If loyalty is defined as being faithful to a cause, ideal, custom, institution or product, then there seems to be a certain amount of infidelity in the workplace these days.

What are the contemporary indicators of the so called 'Infidelity in the Workplace'?

A. Employee Attrition Indicators:

1. One in three employees, the survey says, plans to leave his or her job by the end of the year.

2. 76% of full-time workers, while not actively looking for a new job, would leave their current workplace if the right opportunity came along.

3. the average company loses anywhere from 20% to 50% of its employee base.

B. Employee Aspirations and Dissatisfaction:

1. employees are clearly feeling disconnected from their work.

2. during the recession, companies laid off huge swaths of their employees with little regard for loyalty or length of service

3. a whittling away of benefits, training and promotions for those who remain

4. a generation of young millennials (ages 15 to 30) who have a different set of expectations about their careers, including the need to "be their own brand," wherever it takes them.

One of the casualties is a decreasing sense of commitment to the organization.

C. Fair Treatment and Reciprocity:

1. "When you are talking about loyalty in the workplace, you must think about it as a reciprocal exchange,"

2. "My loyalty to the firm is contingent on my firm's loyalty to me. But there is one party in that exchange which has tremendously more power, and that is the firm."

3. "At a minimum loyalty is not something a company can

rely on. But when people say that employees have no loyalty to their firms, you get into a chicken-and-egg kind of argument. Imagine a different world where firms took care of their employees, and loyalty was reciprocal"

Would employees be job hopping to the extent they are now?"

- Employee behavior, it is said has been influenced by the dramatic organizational restructuring that began 30 years ago. "Firms have always laid off workers, but in the 1980s, you started to see healthy firms laying off workers, mainly for shareholder value."

- In their announcements of pending staff cutbacks, "firms would say, 'We are doing this in the long-term interest of our shareholders, You would also see cuts in employee benefits — e.g.401(k)s instead of defined benefit pensions, and health care costs being pushed on to employees'.

- The trend was toward having the risks be borne by workers instead of firms. If I'm an employee, that's a signal to me that I'm not going to let firms control my career."

- Employers' attitude toward their employees has changed. They see them as short-term resources and because employers have ended lifetime employment, the Skills Gap and what Companies can do About It, job security depends now on continuing usefulness to the employer.

- Cuts in pay and increasing workloads happen when it is useful to the organization. As employees see their careers operating across many employers, they no longer focus their attention solely on the ones they work for now.

Loyalty to Individuals, Not the Company

When we define loyalty, it is "employees being committed to the success of the organization and believing that working for this organization is their best option….. [Loyal employees] they do not actively search for alternative employment and are not responsive to offers. "Employee loyalty" is a "practitioner term. The closest analogy in research is with the concept of commitment, [the idea] that employees are looking after the interests of their employer."

Employee Loyalty is said to be "One piece is having the employer's best interests at heart. The other piece is remaining with the same employer rather than moving on. "Management experts describe this as "organizational commitment." This is changing. "There is less a sense that organization is going to look after you in the way that it used to — which would lead you to expect a reduction in loyalty as well."

"Employees are often more loyal to those around them — their manager, their colleagues, maybe their clients. These employees have a sense of professionalism — and loyalty — that relates to the work they do more than to the company."

If we compare independent contractors to full-time employees we would typically expect these independent contractors to have an "arm's length, less-committed relationship" with company managers compared to the commitment level of full-time staff, he says. "But when I talk to managers, they often suggest that there really isn't much difference between the contractors and the company employees." Relationships with organizations are getting weaker, "why some people believe that company loyalty is dead."

First things first: Where employees are concerned, loyalty has nothing to do with blind obedience, or unthinking devotion, or length of tenure.

Surprised? Think

! Which employee/s display greater loyalty?

1. The employee who has been with you for ten years and in that time, has learned to do just enough to fly, unseen, under the performance issues radar, or

2. The employee who has been with you for 18 months and believes in where you're going, how you want to get there – and proves it every day by her actions Of course experience is important, but given the choice I'll take the employee behind door #2 every time. Truly loyal employees are not just committed to helping their companies succeed; their loyalty is also displayed in other ways, some of them surprising.

1. They display loyalty through integrity and ethical behaviour.

2. They generate discussions others will not care about.

3. They praise their peers.

4. They dissent and disagree at times.

5. They provide support publicly.

6. They are cogent/ frank and tell you what you least want to hear.

7. They leave when they need to leave.

If you can't tell by now, a truly loyal employee is almost always a sensational employee. Often, they're your best employees – so the last thing you want is for them to leave. Yet sometimes they do: For a different lifestyle, for a better opportunity, for a chance to move to a different industry, or simply to take what they've learned and start their own company.

When it's time, they tell you it's time to leave – and they help you prepare to fill the hole they create.

You? You're disappointed but you wish them well. For a time, even if only for a few years, they put your company's interests ahead of their own... ...and now it's your turn to do the same for them.

Of course, you can always make your most convincing arguments to encourage them to stay (hey, you're loyal too!) – but if it doesn't work out, the right thing to do is to return their loyalty, wish them well and help them continue to stay awesome.

C-Suite Mentor Diary 9
Who and What is Mentoring?
What are the Different Types of mentors?

The Dictionary meaning of Mentor is

Mentor: गुरू (Guru - a wise and trusted guide and advisor) The verbs are Mentored: mentored Mentoring: मॉनिटरींग (Do Monitoring) Mentors: मार्गदर्शन (Show a Path) In Marathi it means सल्लागार (Advisor) गुरू (Guru (☐☐☐☐☐☐☐ भाग घेणारी व्यक्ती (Someone who participates in a Council- serve as a teacher or trusted counselor).

The different ways the word Mentor is used gives you a clear idea of what a Mentor stands for/ What he does or does not do.

For e.g.

"It's a tale of the teacher mentor and student who learn from each other, but only in part."

"He was her friend and mentor until his death." – Life Time Mentor.

"Back in Rome, he met Polybius, who became his friend and his mentor in preparing him for a public career." Career Mentor.

"He was a great mentor and friend and he will be sadly missed by everyone who was lucky enough to know him well." Friendly Mentor.

"There is also a new mentor program linking young people to

adults to develop positive relationships outside their peer group." Ice Breaker Mentor.

"But finding a guide, a coach, a friend, a mentor and a support unit, all wrapped up in the one person, is not going to be easy." Searching a Mentor.

"His father is more than a customer, however, serving as a mentor and adviser to Daly. "Customer Mentor

"The latter was his mentor and friend, for whose editorial skills he always retained sincere admiration." Look Up to Mentor.

"It will not even allow me to say that I have been the best mentor and example for students, but I have always tried to be." Idol Mentor.

"He was very encouraging and since then he has become a mentor and friend." Affirmation Mentor.

"After four sessions with his mentor, the student was able to pass the course." Tutor Mentor.

"He became my mentor and good friend and he was one of the world's great authorities on ... "Authority Mentor

The Mentor program

"Under the terms of the Trust, a mentor is to be provided for the successful students to assist and support them during their time at college." Official Mentor

"She's a very dear friend and a great mentor and I really look up to her." Peer Mentor

"He was a kind, gracious, and generous friend, and a mentor

beyond compare. "He was her friend and mentor until his death in 1915. Friendly Mentor.

"He is our mentor, our guide, and he possesses an intellect the size of a planet". Advisor Mentor.

"As the report describes, the mentor program has contributed to the career advancement of protégé' ". Succession Plan Mentor

"A good mentor can help a student or practitioner sort through the options and make decisions". Management or.

www.ingramcontent.com/pod-product-compliance
Lightning Source LLC
Chambersburg PA
CBHW041257180526
45172CB00003B/878